CW00601562

Computer
Hates Me

My Computer Hates Me

Caleb March

BØXTREE

First published 2000 by Boxtree
an imprint of Macmillan Publishers Ltd
25 Eccleston Place London SW1W 9NF
Basingstoke and Oxford

www.macmillan.co.uk

Associated companies throughout the world

ISBN 0 7522 7175 X

Copyright © 2000 Caleb March

The right of Caleb March to be identified as the author of this
work has been asserted by him in accordance with the Copyright,
Designs and Patents Act 1988.

All rights reserved. No part of this publication may be
reproduced, stored in or introduced into a retrieval system,
or transmitted, in any form, or by any means (electronic,
mechanical, photocopying, recording or otherwise) without the
prior written permission of the publisher. Any person who does
any unauthorized act in relation to this publication may be liable
to criminal prosecution and civil claims for damages.

9 8 7 6 5 4 3 2 1

A CIP catalogue record for this book is available from
the British Library.

Designed by Dan Newman/Perfect Bound
Printed by Caledonian

This book is sold subject to the condition that it shall not,
by way of trade or otherwise, be lent, re-sold, hired out,
or otherwise circulated without the publisher's prior consent
in any form of binding or cover other than that in which
it is published and without a similar condition including this
condition being imposed on the subsequent purchaser.

Foreword

Do you need a manual to understand
Word for Dummies? Do you think
software is a warm pair of socks?
Are you not surprised the universal
language turned out to be porn? Then
My Computer Hates Me is for you. Fun,
easy, informative and accessible . . . are
just some of the words Internet Service
Providers will use to con you into signing
up with them. You'll learn all about the
Net — and how it's run by a million virtual-
timeshare salesmen. PC or not PC? The true
meaning of the term geek? They're all in
here. If you thought thirty-two kilobytes of
RAM is what happens if you stroll into a
field full of bulls, then this book is for you.

**System requirements:
One pair eyes,
one pair hands and a sense
of humour.**

**There will be a short
delay while these jokes
load up . . .**

You know you're computer illiterate when . . .

you need a manual to understand Word for Dummies.

...and you think software is a nice warm jumper.

scream

pray

Look around.

If none of your friends
are computer geeks — then
it's probably you.

Since the 1970s

computers have saved acres
of office space — which is now
filled with computers.

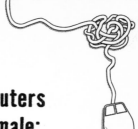

Computers are male:

impossible to figure out and there's never enough memory.

The Computer Geek

shall inherit the earth.

Web site address for vandals:

www.slash-slash-slash-
and-burn.com

Checking your

e-mails more than twice a day
is a sign that it's time
to get out more.

By law,
all Internet
Service Providers must
be described in print as 'easy,
accessible, fun and
affordable'.

The Net was not

created so everyone
could get free access to porn.
It was created for the military
. . . so that they could get free
access to porn.

bomb

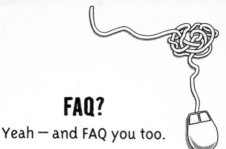

FAQ?

Yeah — and FAQ you too.

E-mail

is a Greek term, meaning
'irrelevant message'.

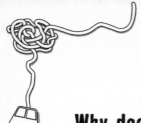

Why does Word

offer misshapen fonts?
You don't need your text to
look like cut-out bits of
newspaper unless you're
planning on kidnapping
someone.

14

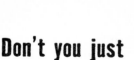

Don't you just

know the terms 'hard', 'floppy' and 'laptop' were created by fans of the Carry On movies?

How come the

only time you remember to back up all your files is when you've just lost all your files?

scream

15

pray

What is it with

'this program has performed an illegal operation'? It's not like your PC went to Buenos Aires and whipped out someone's kidney.

16

Spiders have Web sites.

What we have is a hard-to-locate electronic page of irrelevant information.

The Luddites

had a Web site but they broke it.

17

Who'd have thought

the universal world
language would turn
out to be porn?

The Victorians

used to write to one another
up to five times a day, which
is almost as much as we
e-mail today. This is
progress?

crash

18

swear

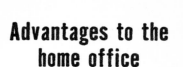

Advantages to the home office

Your PC is unlikely to bring
a sexual harassment case.
Yet.

98%

of all computer errors exist
between keyboard and chair.

scream

pray

ISDN:

It Still Does Nothing.

DOS:

Defective Operating System.

IBM:

I Blame Microsoft.

Computers are like women:

you always imagine there's a better one around the corner.

You never forget

your first computer game.

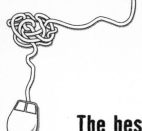

The best thing

about the Internet is it
stops you from staring at a TV
screen all hours of the day
and night.

Computers are female:

every tiny mistake is
automatically committed
to memory.

Dew knot

tryst your spellchecker four
very little thing.

Computer graffiti
'Windows 2000 is just another pane.'

Do magicians and witches
use a spell-checker?

24

Why can't
we back up our minds
onto disk?

Technology?
Big deal. Everyone knows 40%
of all statistics are useless.

25

I don't know

about saving files, but I'll pray for them if you like.

To err is human

but to really screw things up just let a computer loose on the problem.

crash

26

swear

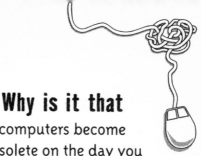

Why is it that

computers become
obsolete on the day you
figure out how to use them?

Silicon Valley:

the laptop of the gods.

Computers won't

be as good as books
until they make one that
you can read in the bath.

Why was Adam

the first computer nerd?
Because he took the
Apple, Mac.

Don't you find

it annoying to be
outsmarted by a
household appliance?

Is 2000

the Year of the Mouse?

Computers are like air-conditioners.

Open the Windows and they stop working properly.

Why doesn't Microsoft build cars?

Because you don't want an airbag that goes 'Are you sure?' before deploying.

31

It's time to shut down the PC for a while when . . .

you decide to read a book but don't know how to boot it up.

32

How many Technical Support Engineers does it take to change a light bulb?

None. All our operatives are busy right now.

33

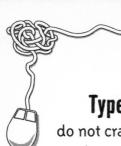

Typewriters

do not crash, don't need
to reboot and don't point
out every tiny little error.

On the eighth day

God made computers. He does
not provide technical
support.

34

Internet Porn:

World Wide Wank.

You know you've

been surfing porn too much
when someone mentions
Silicon Valley and you can
only think of Eva Herzigova's
chest.

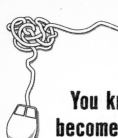

You know you've become a computer nerd when . . .

someone's discussing their worst computer date and you chip in with 'Yeah, mine was 31.12.99.'

. . . your WPM typing rate is higher than your IQ.

. . . you become confused
by that bright yellow
orb in the sky.

. . . you reckon you could've
cured HAL's glitch in a jiffy.

. . . and you think that 2001
was a training film.

Office 2000:
just like a real office —
full of useless commands
and operations.

24-Hour
Internet banking:
because you really want
to know how little you have
at 3 a.m.

crash

38

swear

GEEK:
Greet **E**vil **E**lectronic **K**ing.

If you crash
on the Information
Superhighway, do you call
Auto Recovery?

 39

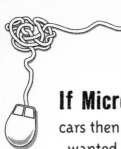

If Microsoft made

cars then whenever you
wanted the radio on,
you'd have to turn off the
engine first.

The setting is
de fault.

bomb

hate

Each new generation

of computers is more
compact and well defined.
The opposite is true
of their users.

Your computer needs upgrading if . . .

instead of pounds, it has a symbol for groats.

. . . and it's running Leaded Windows.

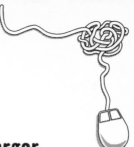

The larger
the font
the smaller
the idea.

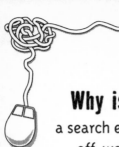

Why isn't there
a search engine for day-off-work excuses?

In cyberspace
no one can tell if you're clean.

44

You know you're addicted to the Net . . .

when each month is a decision
whether to pay the mortgage
or the phone bill . . . and you
can't remember what a
mortgage is.

Why isn't there
a package called
Microsoft Office Amateur?

Sign on CD-ROM:
game requires 100 MHz
Pentium processor,
16MB RAM and gullible
teenager.

46

The trouble with
cyber-babes is they won't
put out unless they're
pixelated.

Heard about
the temp who Tippexed out
her mistakes on the monitor?

47

Surfing the Net

is like looking for the
Holy Grail.
Correction: Holey Gail.

WEB PAGE:

Wholly **E**xtraneous **B**aloney
Pertaining to **A** **G**iant **E**go.

bomb

hate

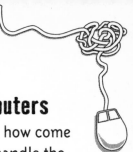

If computers

are so great, how come
they can't handle the
smallest little magnet?

If you're recovering

from Internet addiction, do
you go on a twelve-click
program?

49

The best game
is the one where you're
at the helm of the Enterprise
and all the stars are coming at
you out of space.
I think they call it
Screensaver.

crash

swear

Remember when
a busy server used to be
an overworked waiter?

**Heard about the
virtual Trappist
monastery?**
There's no chat room.

scream

pray

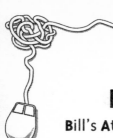

BASIC:
Bill's Attempt to Seize
Industry Control.

Once you have
your menus up and running,
you'll never see a real one
again.

bomb

52

hate

Bill Gates:

the man who thinks he's IT.

The pocket computer

In one simple movement you
can lose your address book,
your first novel, your joke
database and any semblance
of a life.

cry

freeze

WINDOWS:

Will **I**nstall **N**eedless **D**ata **O**n **W**hole **S**ystem.

Isn't forward slash,

forward slash, back slash what you do after a night's heavy drinking?

crash

54

swear

Your spell-checker

is not as effective as think.

Surfing the Web

is like looking for a clitoris.
You spend for ever trying to
find it and when you do, you
wonder what all the fuss was
all about.

scream

pray

Faxes
are like e-mails from the
1980s.

The time to get
worried is when you receive
an e-mail beginning:
'Greetings, Earthling . . .'
And it's not from your
X-Files .alt group.

E-mail:
communication by
word of mouse.

Net etiquette:
a guide to modem manners.

57

Why does your
Service Provider tell you
that 'we' are experiencing
some problems when they
mean 'you'?

Basic Computer
Language:
Smash forehead on keyboard
to continue.

crash

swear

How do I
set my laser printer
to 'stun'?

The bigger the font,
the smaller the contents of
your report.

People the Net doesn't need:

Those who start up
newsgroups with names like
alt.stunt.cock.
. . . or who create perversions
so weird they haven't even
got their own Web site.
. . . or who start this week's
virus rumour.

bomb

hate

Fans of Tomb Raider:

Star Croft Lovers.

Twenty-first-century literature:

Cyber with Rosie.
Pride and Processors.

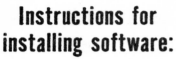

Instructions for installing software:

Run Install; check Internet connection, register user name and password . . . reboot system. Fetch six-year-old to start again properly.

Psycho Web site:

Http forward-slash
forward-slash.www.
gurgle.eek.eek.eek.

You know you're

spending too long surfing
porn if you can't even hold on
to a virtual relationship.

scream

63

pray

America On Line:
Super Information
Highway robbery.

Memo to USA teen chat room users:
OK. Marilyn Manson rules,
now log off!

64

Cyber pups are not house-trained.

They will leave dead batteries
in your hall.

If you get caught

for Internet crime, will you
end up sewing e-mail bags?

cry

freeze

Surfing the Web

isn't like surfing at all. Not
even if you stand on your
ironing board.

IT has caused

a huge growth industry —
in selling manuals on
how to use IT.

Along with Word for Dummies,

there is now HTML for Morons and Windows for Arseholes.

Moving the porn

down from the top shelf
and onto a screen in front
of you is not really progress,
is it?

68

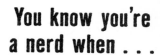

You know you're
a nerd when . . .

you and your friends get all
dewy-eyed remembering the
Spectrum ZX80.
And you haven't got any
friends.

cry

freeze

The fear of

viruses and bugs has been
very overratwofr9hbv8yfd.

You're computer
illiterate . . .

if you think a high resolution
is something you make on
New Year's Eve.

crash

swear

You know technology
is taking over when your
PC asks for the e-mail
address of that sexy little
Pentium at the office.

71

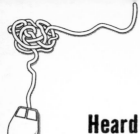

Heard about

the latest PC game that
takes ages to install then
eats your memory?
It's called Alzheimer's.

If your screen

informs you that you have insufficient funds, look around you — you could be standing in front of a cashpoint.

Amish Web site:

http//_____

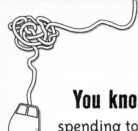

You know you're

spending too long at the
screen when you can't think
of ten friends to copy that
chain e-mail on to.

How did we ever

waste time before e-mail, the
Net and PC games?

crash

swear

The Internet is

thirty years old — but let's
see it blow out a candle.

Does God think
he's Bill Gates?

75

UPGRADE:
User **P**urchases **GRA**dually
Disintegrating **E**quipment.

How to tell you've got a senile PC:
it's grey, it's slow and it has
no memory.

To continue, press any key.
No . . . NOT THAT ONE!

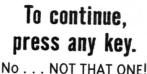

The Net is like a handbag:
mysterious, ever-expanding and no one has any idea what you'll find in there.

cry

freeze

'By reading these instructions, you agree to accept and honour Microsoft as your one true saviour. Repent all ye who "Enter" here.'

78

Only perfect spellers

are welcome to log in.

A journey

of a thousand sites begins
with one click.

79

If you get

an error message, a
query about saving the file
and your printer won't print —
it's time to start questioning
whether the work is any good
or not.

bomb

A computer is like a penis:

once you start playing with it, it's hard to stop.

The Net is like sex:

Without the right protective measures it can spread viruses.

Only three things

are certain in this world.
Death, taxes and lost files.

Oh, what a tangled
Web site we weave.

Give a man a fish

and he will feed himself
for one day. Give him the
Net and he'll be off your
hands for at least a month.

The modem

is the message.

A computer is like a penis #2:

Those who have one think they're superior to those that don't. Those that don't can't see what the fuss is about over a silly toy. And yet many of those that don't have one spend a lot of time trying to access one.

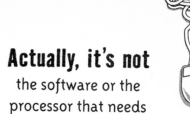

Actually, it's not

the software or the
processor that needs
upgrading — it's you.

The Web:

A bazaar where you'll find
everything but what you
came in for.

85

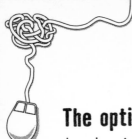

The optimist says

the glass is half full, the pessimist says the glass is half empty. The computer engineer says the container is twice the size it needs to be.

When are they

going to release the
strategy guide to life?

It's not the size

of the hard disk;
it's what's on it that counts.

You can't teach
an old mouse new clicks.

Too many clicks
spoil the browse.

Programmer's maxim:

User = Loser.

E-mail:

because I really need a tenth-
generation virus warning that
begins with yards of headers
of the other nerds who have
received it.

User-friendly:
a term to describe software that makes perfect sense to a computer programmer.

If the CC list
is longer than the contents of the message then it doesn't need to be sent.

crash

swear

Confuse a nerd:
tell him The X-Files is real —
but everything else isn't!

Who needs
Internet cafés?
You get a different order to
the one you asked for and
your server is still busy for
forty minutes.

scream

91

pray

Usenet groups:
A site for four eyes.

An expert:
someone who breaks other people's computers.

The 'Forward' and 'CC'

buttons on your e-mail toolbar are designed for bad jokes, gossip and improbable hoax warnings.

On the seventh day,

Bill rested (and still made $50m).

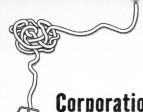

Corporations do not
do business via chain-letter
and Microsoft is not
offering money to 'test a
new product'. Welcome to
hoax e-mail.

A printer consists of
three parts. Case, blinking red
light, jammed paper tray.

Hardware:

the collective term for
anything that can be kicked,
punched or bitten.

An error message:

a short confusing remark
blaming the user instead of
the software.

scream

pray

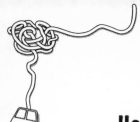

Help:

a feature used to generate more questions. If used correctly, you can navigate through a whole series of queries to arrive back where you started.

Programmers

used to be geeks who spoke Klingon. Now they're so rich they hire people to speak Klingon for them.

Imagine if . . .

every time you moved a
file, it suddenly turned up
in another filing cabinet with
a different name? No, this is
not Kafka — this is
technology.

crash

swear

Collective nouns:

A click of chat room users.
A mouse of programmers.
A slow of tech. support.

PC or not PC.

Are you sure that's the
question?

99

More twenty-first-century literature:

Catcher in the RAM.
Brave New Word.
Lord of the Files.
A Clockwork Apple.
The Bill Gates of Perception.
Of Mice and Men.

100

How come

role-playing fantasy
games never ask you to
imagine that you're a spotty
adolescent from Droitwich?

The biggest influence

on computer game design is
old YES album covers.

cry

freeze

The Web is chaotic,

unmanageable and there's
no one in charge. Not
surprising, then, that it was
designed by a Brit.

You're computer illiterate if . . .

you think fully specced means you just paid a visit to the optician.

Greatest piece of computer fiction:

the product manuals.

PC games are like Christmas.

Lots of big boxes with very little in them.

How to tell if your computer's too old:

The documents are in copperplate.

Microsoft alchemy:

Silicon into gold.

By law, all
multimedia games must feature thrones, chalices, swords, damsels and at least one glitch for which you'll need a cheat code.

Telecottaging:
working from bed.

Elderly parents.

Start your own Web site. You're guaranteed more visits from strangers than from your ungrateful offspring — and you can e-mail them to complain about it too!

Now we have the fastest, most efficient PCs, all we need now is something to help us to remember our passwords.

If we'd wanted secrets, we'd never have created the Internet.

108

Get into the Guinness Book of Records

by being the person kept waiting the longest by technical support (current record: 3 weeks, 5 days, 16 hours and 47 minutes).

cry

freeze

Your computer's hidden settings:

Crash every [2] hours.
Server fails on every [4]th try.
Slow down system loading by
[10] times.

If your Web-addict

support group has an e-mail
address, they aren't trying
hard enough.

Frivolous e-mails

include jokes, gossip, bitching and amusing usage of font, bold and italics . . . hang on, that's all of them.

You're using your

computer too much if you have to de-fluff your mouse more than three times a year.

It's time to worry

about your cyber-lover
when your e-mail Valentine
has been CC'd to five other
people.

Windows 69.

The system you actually hope
will go down on you.

bomb

hate

You know you're too old for computers when . . .

you think a hard drive is what happens on the first tee.

. . . you're still making that joke about roadkill and the information superhighway.

. . . you approach a computer brandishing a crank handle.

cry

113

freeze

If computers

are so smart, how come
they can't tell you where
you left your keys?

Computers in films

make noises when a program
is complete. Real computers
only make a noise when
something is wrong.

The difference between PC users and convicts:

PC users use Windows to get to their files. Convicts use files to get through their windows.

Wherever I lay my @, that's my home.

How many Microsoft engineers does it take to change a light bulb?

None. Bill Gates will simply make darkness the new industry standard.

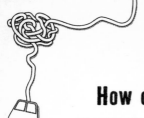

How come

your computer can
automatically change its
clock for GMT, but it can't
handle Y2K?

How to make money

on the Web. Start a Web site
for Web addicts.

crash

swear

Why computers are dull:

No great binary jokes. (Not even 101001100010010.)

CD-ROM:

Consumer Device — Rendered Obsolete in Months.

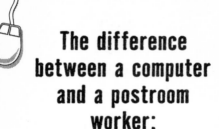

The difference between a computer and a postroom worker:

With the computer you only have to punch the information in once.

The problem

with real life is that when things go wrong, you can't just pop outside, ring the bell and start all over again.

Return:

what you do with a computer once you've bought it.

Modern nursery rhymes:

'Alice in Windowland'
'Three Blind Mice'
'Little Miss Microsoft'

One day there

will be Windows 666 — but
it'll be a devil to install.

E-mail:
hundreds more ways to be snubbed in business!

How soon
before we get Internet shoplifting?

scream

123

pray

When to get paranoid about your PC:

Your e-mails are returned addressee unknown, your 'office assistant' starts bitching about you and your new password is Mr Tiny Brain.

bomb

When it comes to devising computer games . . .

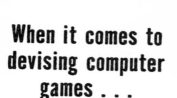

there's no way you can make the word 'educational' sound more exciting than 'racing' or 'killing'.

Computers age in dog years.

The older they get the slower they are to respond to commands.

crash

swear

Why is a millennium-compliant computer like a great night out?

You get four digits in your date.

Caleb March was first booted up in 1965 and expects to have crashed by the time you read this. Schooled in Silicon Valley, he majored in data analysis, word processing and profuse lying. He was all for Betamax in the eighties, IBM in the nineties and is now looking into several thousand Internet adult retail sites. He joined Microsoft in 1993 and was quickly promoted to the board, until he used it for windsurfing. Now a program debugger (removing those put in by the manufacturers), his hobbies are game-playing, junk culture and insulting strangers in binary. He is currently recovering from Internet addiction on a twelve-click programme.

bomb

hate